JOURNEY TO MARS

MISSION: MARS

CHERRY LAKE PRESS

Published in the United States of America by Cherry Lake Publishing
Ann Arbor, Michigan
www.cherrylakepublishing.com

Reading Adviser: Beth Walker Gambro, MS, Ed., Reading Consultant, Yorkville, IL
Book Designer: Book Buddy Media
Photo Credits: cover: ©NASA / nasa.gov; page 1: ©Alones / Shutterstock; page 5: ©NASA/JPL/ USGS / nasa.gov; page 7: ©ESA/NASA / nasa.gov; page 9: ©NASA / nasa.gov; page 10: ©NASA / nasa.gov; page 13: ©SpaceX / nasa.gov; page 15: ©NASA/JPL-Caltech / nasa.gov; page 16: ©NASA/JPL-Caltech / nasa.gov; page 19: ©NASA / nasa.gov; page 21: ©nasa.gov; page 23: ©Carmen Martínez Torrón / Getty Images; page 25: ©NASA/JPL / nasa.gov; page 27: ©NASA / nasa.gov; page 28: ©Nisian Hughes / Getty Images; page 29: ©Spencer Platt / Staff / Getty Images; page 30: ©Anton Petrus / Getty Images

Cherry Lake Press is an imprint of Cherry Lake Publishing Group.

Library of Congress Cataloging-in-Publication Data has been filed and is available at catalog.loc.gov

Cherry Lake Publishing would like to acknowledge the work of the Partnership for 21st Century Learning, a Network of Battelle for Kids. Please visit *http://www.battelleforkids.org/networks/p21* for more information.

Printed in the United States of America
Corporate Graphics

ABOUT THE AUTHOR

Mari Bolte is a children's book author and editor. Streaming sci-fi on TV is more her speed but tracking our planet's progress across the sky is still exciting! She lives in Minnesota with her husband, daughter, and a house full of (non-Martian) pets.

TABLE OF CONTENTS

Destination: Mars

Around 4.5 billion years ago, our solar system was a nebula, or a cloud made of gas and dust. Then the nebula collapsed. It spun into a flat disk shape. Tiny bits of space dust from the nebula began to form and lump together. Most of the dust was pulled to the center of the disk and became the Sun.

The rest of the dust began to clump together, first into small pieces and then bigger and bigger balls. Some of those balls are what we know today as **asteroids** or **comets**. Other balls became moons and planets. One of those planets is Mars.

Mars is home to the biggest canyon and the largest volcano in our solar system.

At 142 million miles (228 million kilometers) away, Mars is the fourth planet from the Sun. It is the second-smallest planet in our solar system. And it is a terrestrial planet. Terrestrial planets are made of rocks or metal. Earth, Venus, and Mercury are terrestrial planets too. This means they have a dense, metallic **core**, a rocky layer called the mantle, and a thin outer layer called the crust.

Other than Earth, no planet has been explored more than Mars. Living on Mars is still just an idea, but it is one that is coming closer to reality every day. National Aeronautics and

One-Way Ticket

Probes are spacecraft that travel through space and gather information. They do not carry people. They send what they learn back to Earth for scientists to study. The United States launched its first probe, Explorer 1, *on January 31, 1958.* Explorer 1 *flew in a looping path that ranged as far as 1,594 miles (2,565 km) from Earth. Today, that distance seems like a walk across the park! On May 11, 2021, Voyager 1 reached a distance of 14 billion miles (24 billion km) away from Earth.* Voyager 1 *launched in 1977 and has been flying through space ever since. Who knows how many miles it will travel?*

Space Administration (NASA) scientists have nearly 60 years of experience exploring Mars with spacecraft. Many of these spacecraft, including, including **orbiters** and rovers, have already made the journey to the Red Planet. Rovers are motor vehicles specially designed to travel across the surface of Mars. *Perseverance*, a rover currently on a mission on Mars, is working to pave the way for human life beyond Earth.

NASA astronauts are getting experience living off-planet too. People from more than 40 nations have spent more than 50,000 combined days in space so far. The things they learn about living in Earth's orbit can be used when humans explore Mars. NASA's goal is to send humans to the Moon again by 2024. Then, Mars awaits!

Astronaut Tim Peake spent 185 days, 22 hours, and 11 minutes in space. He was the first British astronaut from the European Space Agency (ESA) to visit the ISS.

Thrills on Mars

In 2015, British astronaut Tim Peake became the first man to complete a marathon, or a 26.2-mile (42.2 km) race—in space! Peake had to wear a harness to strap himself to the treadmill. Sometimes the harness was uncomfortable. Getting enough nutrients to run is important, but eating and drinking was also a challenge for Peake. On Earth, the food you eat sits in your stomach. Even then, runners sometimes get sick to their stomachs. In space, food floats around, even inside of you! Peake had to plan his pre-race meal carefully. In the end, he finished the race from the International Space Station (ISS) in 3 hours, 35 minutes, and 21 seconds.

CHAPTER 2

Traveling Through Space

The contest to dominate space began in the mid-1950s between the United States and Russia. The countries were already in an arms race, with both sides rushing to make the biggest, scariest bombs, weapons, and ammunition. The race to see who could be the first to claim space seemed like a natural next step.

In 1957, the Russians launched *Sputnik*, an orbiting **satellite**. The United States was not far off, sending *Explorer 1* into orbit just a few months later. In 1958, NASA was formed. The United States was serious about space exploration.

International Space Station

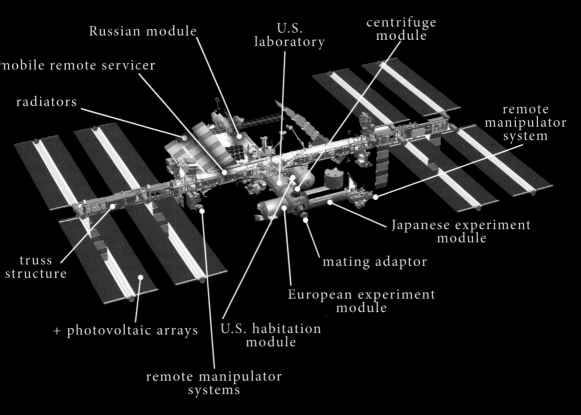

Russian module
U.S. laboratory
centrifuge module
mobile remote servicer
radiators
remote manipulator system
truss structure
+ photovoltaic arrays
U.S. habitation module
remote manipulator systems
European experiment module
mating adaptor
Japanese experiment module

- The ISS orbits about 250 miles (402 km) above Earth. If you look at the stars at night, you will be able to see it. It is the third-brightest object in the sky!

- Eight spaceships can dock at the ISS at one time.

- Spacecraft from Earth can reach the ISS in as few as 3 hours.

- The ISS is about the size of a football field. Usually between three and six astronauts from various countries are aboard at any time.

The ISS is the third-brightest object in the sky, after the Sun and Moon. From Earth, it can be seen without a telescope. It looks like a fast-moving plane in the sky.

NASA has led the space race ever since. Today, more than half of the spacecraft orbiting Earth belong to the United States.

The United States is not the only country interested in space travel. Nine countries and one international organization have the ability to launch spacecraft. A number of other countries, such as Canada and Italy, have space programs but must use launch systems in other countries. Thirty-eight countries own or operate objects that orbit Earth. But all of those countries work together aboard the ISS.

Twin Tested

An average stay on the ISS is about 6 months. But it takes longer than that to get to Mars! The longest visit to the ISS by an American was by Scott Kelly in 2016. He was there for 340 days. And Kelly gave NASA even more to study because he has a twin brother, Mark. This gave scientists a rare opportunity to gauge how astronauts are affected by being in space. Scientists were able to compare how Scott was affected, both mentally and physically, and compare this to his **genetically** identical twin on Earth. When Scott returned from the ISS, scientists noticed some of his genes had changed a little. They were particularly concerned about the genes that affect the immune system. Scientists do not yet know if the changes mean anything. But they will keep monitoring both twins.

The first piece of the ISS was launched from a Russian rocket in 1998. By 2000, the ISS was ready for astronauts to arrive. The first crew landed on November 2. More pieces have been added to the space station since then. The final piece of the ISS was added in 2011. Today, NASA, Russia's Roscosmos, Japan's **Aerospace** Exploration Agency, the Canadian Space Agency, and the European Space Agency all contribute astronauts to the ISS crews.

Early Check-In

One piece of the ISS is called the Bigelow Expandable Activity Module. The module didn't take up much space on a rocket. Once it was **deployed** in space, it expanded into a full **habitat**, like a balloon. The module is being studied now to see how it holds up in space. Some believe the modules could pave the way for space tourism. That means hotels in space and on Mars could be in the future. Outer space and Mars's surface are not the most comfortable of places. But, if resorts on Earth are any clue to what people like, fancy places to be pampered in space will be a necessity. Hotels, spas, and wellness centers might be key to staying physically and mentally healthy so far from home.

The ISS has taught us what living in outer space is like. NASA astronauts have stepped onto the Moon. It is only natural that Mars would be the next target. The journey to Mars is like a race too. Only this time, the race is between NASA and private companies.

Billionaire Richard Branson's Virgin Galactic has been sending rocket-powered planes to 50 miles (80.5 km) above Earth, the edge of space. Hundreds of people have spent between $250,000 and $450,000 apiece for the chance to ride on his spaceplane in the future. Branson himself traveled into space on his own aircraft on July 11, 2021. The flight lasted about 60 minutes. Branson hopes to eventually offer 400 flights a year.

On February 6, 2018, SpaceX sent its first rocket into space. A mannequin, called Starman, was put in a cherry-red Tesla Roadster. Then the Roadster was attached to the rocket. Starman is on an asymmetrical orbit around the Sun.

Businessman Jeff Bezos owns a rocket company called Blue Origin. His plan is to send people into space to live and work. On July 20, 2021, Bezos and three crewmates took a 10-minute flight to space on Blue Origin's *New Shepard* rocket. The crew, which included the youngest and oldest people ever to go into space, were in space for 10 minutes and 10 seconds.

SpaceX, owned by **entrepreneur** Elon Musk, has been the most vocal about **colonizing** Mars. SpaceX has sent internet satellites into orbit. It has delivered packages and people to the ISS. Its goal is to send a crewed flight to Mars by 2026.

CHAPTER 3

X Marks the Spot

Every journey to Mars has inspired new inventions and new technology. Scientists can try out the latest ideas on a small scale on Mars before sending a bigger version later. For example, the first rover, *Sojourner*, landed in 1997. It weighed just 23 pounds (10.4 kilograms). *Perseverance* landed in 2021. It weighs 2,260 pounds (1,025 kg)!

We know from photos what Mars looks like. But what does it sound like? Microphones were aboard the *Mars Polar Lander* and the *Phoenix Mars Lander*. The *Polar* mission failed, though. And the microphone on the *Phoenix* was never turned on. But thanks to the *InSight* lander and the rover *Perseverance*, scientists now know!

On December 1, 2018, *InSight Mars Lander* recorded vibrations caused by the wind on Mars. The vibrations were

Perseverance uses artificial intelligence to drive itself across the surface of Mars.

recorded by two tools. One was an air pressure **sensor**, which was there to study the atmosphere. It was able to record the sound of the wind. The other was a seismometer, which was designed to pick up vibrations from marsquakes.

The sound was so exciting that the next rover, *Perseverance*, was sent with actual audio equipment. Specially designed microphones and an amplifier help the rover "hear." The rover sent back sound recordings during the flight to Mars. Once on the planet, it recorded surface sounds, wind, laser impacts on rock, driving sounds, and the *Ingenuity* helicopter in flight.

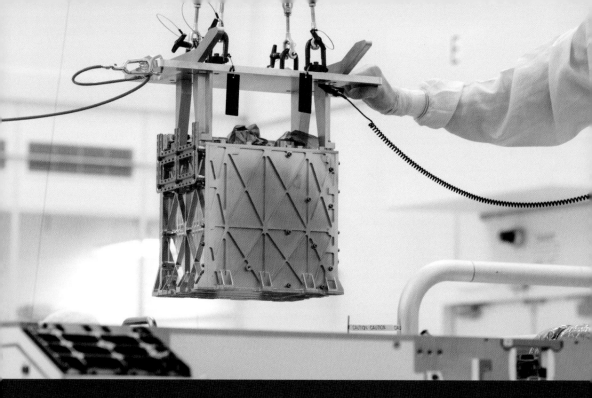

Technicians in the clean room are carefully lowering the MOXIE instrument into the belly of the *Perseverance* rover.

The rover *Perseverance* has a small system on board called the Mars Oxygen In-Situ Resource Utilization Project (MOXIE). MOXIE uses a technique called **electrolysis** to turn carbon dioxide into oxygen. In April 2021, *Perseverance* was able to make oxygen from Mars's atmosphere. It created 5 grams (0.18 ounces) of oxygen. That is only enough for about 10 minutes of breathing. Scientists hope that MOXIE might one day be able to make enough oxygen for colonists and for rocket launches.

Risky Business

Oxygen itself is not flammable, but it can cause a spark that can become a huge fire. Mars does not have a dense enough atmosphere or enough oxygen to create a fire. Astronauts would need to bring stores of oxygen along to survive. In 1970, the Apollo 13 spacecraft was approaching the Moon's orbit. Everything looked fine. Then, the oxygen tanks aboard exploded. One of the tanks was damaged during an earlier test. It could not empty itself of oxygen. Testers thought they had fixed the problem. But their fix did not work. It actually damaged the wires inside the tank. On board the spacecraft, a spark from one of the wires was enough to start a fire, and then an explosion. To prevent this from happening on Mars, fire safety is already being discussed. Buildings are being designed to seal off areas in case of fire.

In December 2020, engineering students at Washington University in St. Louis, Missouri, designed a special machine that can remove hydrogen and oxygen directly from saltwater. It can make 25 times more oxygen than MOXIE, while using the same amount of power. Maybe the next rover or lander will be equipped with this new technology.

Exploring the Planet

Space is already starting to get a little crowded. There are thousands of man-made objects orbiting Earth right now. We use them for **GPS navigation**, weather **forecasting**, and cell phone data. On top of those man-made objects, there is also clutter, such as broken parts from the ISS and the Hubble Space Telescope, spent rocket fuel containers, and hardware like nuts and bolts. There are even millions of bits of plastic and peeled paint.

The RemoveDEBRIS satellite was launched from the ISS in 2018. It was equipped with both a net to collect trash, and a harpoon to stab large pieces. It also had navigation technology to locate space junk.

The objects travel in different directions, orbits, and speeds. Collisions happen all the time. In 2009, two satellites crashed into each other at 22,300 miles (35,888 km) per hour. Both satellites were destroyed, creating thousands of new bits of space clutter.

Earth's gravity makes sure that anything scientists have put in its orbit will eventually fall back down. NASA says at least one piece of clutter returns to Earth every day. But what about the bits that go to Mars?

By the Numbers

Space trash is a big deal! Even a tiny chip of paint can cause a lot of damage.

- *There are more than 8,000 man-made objects orbiting Earth.*
- *At least 23,000 pieces of space junk are softball-size.*
- *More than 500,000 pieces are marble-size, and big enough to end a mission to space. They can damage fuel tanks, spacecraft cabins, and protective systems.*
- *More than 100,000 million pieces are the size of a grain of sand. The pieces move around at speeds between 15,700 and 17,500 miles (25,267 and 28,164 km) per hour.*
- *A single piece could tear a spacesuit or crack a space shuttle window. Pieces as small as 0.04 inch (1 millimeter) pose the highest risks for mission-ending damage.*

We are already taking space junk to Mars. Orbiters circle the planet and send information back to Earth. But not all the orbiters are active. When they stop working, they just stay there. Mars also has two moons in its orbit, Phobos and Deimos. In 2017, the NASA orbiter *MAVEN* looked like it might collide with Phobos. Mission control had to use the orbiter's rocket engine to move it out of the way. On Earth, moving spacecraft off of a crash course is a command that takes just a few seconds. But there is a delay of approximately 13 minutes between commands sent from Earth until they reach Mars. Dodging oncoming traffic there is a little harder!

MAVEN stands for *Mars Atmosphere and Volatile EvolutioN*. It was NASA's tenth Mars orbiter.

Similar Exploration

Earth's oceans are crowded with clutter too. The Great Pacific Garbage Patch in the Pacific Ocean is a huge mass of trash. Most of the patch is made up of plastic that does not disappear. Instead, the plastic breaks up into smaller and smaller pieces. Eventually, they are so small that they are microscopic. Those **microplastics** *end up in our drinking water.*

No one knows how big the Great Pacific Garbage Patch is. Inventors are working hard to think of ways to sort out and remove the plastics from the water. It is so far from any country that no one feels personally responsible.

In 2021, a Japanese company partnered with the United Kingdom's space program. The company had a vision to make space development safe and sustainable for future generations. They wanted to start by cleaning up space debris. What if they had a spacecraft that could attach itself to dead **satellites** with a magnet and docking plates? It could push the satellites toward Earth, where they would burn up in Earth's atmosphere.

Around 8 million tons of plastic end up in oceans around the world every year. Once plastic reaches the ocean, it is hard, or even impossible, to collect.

They launched a test spacecraft. It was two pieces that detached in orbit. One piece would pretend the other piece was space junk and try to find it. If successful, future satellites could be built with docking plates already attached.

The Future

Scientists have made many inventions to prepare us for Mars. Rockets to get there, oxygen-producing rovers, expandable modules, and space cleanup machines are just the start.

Communication is something scientists are always looking to improve. With simple messages and data taking around 13 minutes to be delivered, finding a faster way is important. Laser technology could make that possible. In 2021, a U.S. Space Force satellite will launch to Mars. It will make optical communication possible. Optical communication uses infrared lasers to send and receive information. The lasers are faster than radio waves, and more secure. Scientists could receive real-time information about what rovers—and one day, astronauts—are up to.

[21ST CENTURY SKILLS LIBRARY]

Laser communication will allow 10 to 100 times more information to pass between Mars and Earth. It is much faster than the radio frequencies that are currently being used.

Astronauts will also need a reliable power supply. Some rovers used **solar power**. They collected around 140 watts of power a day. In order to run, the rovers needed about 100 watts of power. This is about the same amount as the lightbulbs in your house. They also had rechargeable batteries, but batteries only last so long. Other rovers use an element called plutonium. Plutonium is a very effective source of energy. Around 2.2 pounds (1 kg) can produce up to 10 million kilowatts of power.

What's Our Responsibility?

*We are learning more about Mars every day. With the technology and resources we have right now, it looks like a Mars colony would be completely dependent on fuel from Earth. The fuel on Earth is not infinite. If we keep using uranium at its current pace, it could all be gone in about 230 years. Plutonium is even more rare. It is also very **radioactive**, which makes handling it dangerous. Pulling resources from Earth to use them on Mars creates an ethical dilemma. Should we spend that time and money on making life on Earth better instead?*

The Kilopower Reactor Using Stirling Technology (KRUSTY) led the way in developing affordable, long-lasting nuclear power for use in outer space.

That's enough electricity to run almost 1,000 houses for a whole year. But our supply of plutonium is not infinite. And it is very expensive to use.

NASA has worked with the U.S. Department of Energy to develop a nuclear reactor power system. It runs off a piece of uranium about the size of a paper towel roll. The system can create 10 kilowatts of electricity for at least 10 years. That much power would easily be enough for a colony on Mars or the Moon.

The first people on Mars will not find life easy. There will be few comforts and it will be hard work to survive.

The journey to Mars has prompted a lot of questions that still need answers. It has also inspired many new ideas and inventions. Thanks to the work of scientists, we have seen new sights and heard new sounds. We have learned what life in space might be like and can already imagine living there ourselves. Pack your bag, book a flight, and wait for the day when science fiction becomes science reality.

Oxygen bars offer a variety of "flavors" for customers to experience while they breathe deeply.

Living on Mars

On Earth, people line up to visit oxygen bars. Customers wear a tube under their noses and breathe in deeply. Their lungs fill with 95 percent pure oxygen. Sometimes a soothing scent, like lemongrass or peppermint, is added. The alleged benefits of an oxygen bar include stress relief, mood enhancement, and headache relief. People really might enjoy being relaxed on Mars too! Oxygen bars, with scents that remind customers of smells back home, might be popular. Martian mud baths, volcanic rock scrubs, and hot Mars stone treatments could be other ways to be soothed in space.

Activity: Earth Junk

Whether it's the Great Pacific Garbage Patch or anywhere out in space, people produce piles of trash. Every day, 3.5 million tons of plastic and waste are created. How much trash do you make in a single day? The amount may surprise you!

WHAT YOU'LL NEED:

- **trash bags**
- **gallon-size zip-top bags**

1. Carry a trash bag with you wherever you go. Every time you have something you would normally throw away, place it in the trash bag instead.

2. If it is food waste, like a can, wrapper, or peel, place it in a zip-top bag. Wash the items first, if you want.

3. If you fill a bag, write your name on it and set it somewhere safe. Then start a new bag.

4. At the end of the day, weigh your trash bag or bags. How much trash did you create? What could you do in the future to reduce the amount of garbage you throw away?

Find Out More

BOOKS

Bearce, Stephanie. *This or That Questions About Space and Beyond: You Decide!* North Mankato, MN: Capstone Press, 2021.

Hand, Carol. *Living in Space.* New York, NY: PowerKids Press, 2021.

Hirsch, Rebecca E. *Space Machines in Action: An Augmented Reality Experience.* Minneapolis, MN: Lerner Publications, 2020.

Owen, Ruth. *Astronauts.* New York, NY: AV2, 2020.

Saxon, Anna. *Scott Kelly: Astronaut Twin Who Spent a Year in Space.* North Mankato, MN: Capstone Press, 2021.

WEBSITES

NASA: International Space Station
https://www.nasa.gov/mission_pages/station/main/index.html
The official NASA page for the latest news, crews, missions, and research aboard the International Space Station.

NASA: Space Debris and Human Spacecraft
https://www.nasa.gov/mission_pages/station/news/orbital_debris.html
Learn about the orbital debris and other "space junk" that circles our planet.

United Nations Office for Outer Space Affairs
https://www.unoosa.org/oosa/en/ourwork/space-agencies.html
Official links to the space programs of every country involved in the United Nations Outer Space Affairs.

Where Is Starman?
https://www.whereisroadster.com
Track Starman and his Tesla Roadster as it travels through space.

GLOSSARY

aerospace (AIR-uh-spays) having to do with aviation and spaceflight

asteroids (AS-tuh-roydz) small rocky bodies in space

colonizing (KOL-uh-nyz-eeng) sending a group of settlers to a new place

comets (KOM-itz) space snowballs made up of frozen gases, rock, and dust; comets orbit the Sun

core (KOR) the innermost layers of a planet; cores can be solid, liquid, or both

deployed (duh-PLOYD) moved something into position

electrolysis (uh-lek-TROL-uh-sys) a technique that is used to change chemicals using electricity

entrepreneur (on-truh-puh-NOOR) a person who operates a business

forecasting (FOR-kasst-eeng) predicting or estimating a future event or trend

genetically (juh-NET-ik-uh-lee) related to the origin of a person or animal's inherited characteristics

GPS navigation (GEE-PEE-ESS nav-uh-GAY-shuhn) a satellite navigation system that uses satellite signals to find a receiver's position on Earth

microplastics (MI-kroh-plas-tikz) extremely small pieces of plastic

orbiters (or-BIT-uhrz) a spacecraft designed to orbit a planet

radioactive (ray-dee-oh-AK-tiv) emitting radiation, a form of energy that travels through space

satellite (SAT-uh-lite) an artificial body placed in orbit

sensor (SEN-sohr) a device that detects or measures changes

solar power (SOH-luhr POW-uhr) power gained by harnessing the energy of the Sun's rays

INDEX